STRANGE HISTORIES
THE EGYPTIANS

Jane Shuter

Chrysalis Children's Books

LOOK FOR THE EYE

Look for the eye in boxes like this. Here you will find extra facts, stories and other interesting information about the strange world of the Egyptians.

First published in the UK in 2003 by
Chrysalis Children's Books
An imprint of Chrysalis Books Group Plc
The Chrysalis Building, Bramley Road,
London W10 6SP

Paperback edition first published in 2005
Copyright © Chrysalis Books Group Plc 2003

Produced by
Monkey Puzzle Media Ltd
Gissing's Farm, Fressingfield
Suffolk IP21 5SH, UK

Designer: Jamie Asher
Editor: Kate Phelps
Picture Research: Lynda Lines

ISBN 1 84138 664 2 (hb)
ISBN 1 84458 252 3 (pb)

British Library Cataloguing in Publication Data for this book is available from the British Library.

Printed in China
10 9 8 7 6 5 4 3 2 1

Acknowledgements
We wish to thank the following individuals and organizations for their help and assistance and for supplying material in their collections: AKG 10 (Erich Lessing), 11 bottom (Erich Lessing), 17 bottom (Erich Lessing; Ancient Art and Architecture Collection front cover and back cover left, 1 (Mary Jelliffe), 4 bottom (R Sheridan), 5 (J Stevens), 6 (R Sheridan), 7 top (R Sheridan), 12 bottom (R Sheridan), 16 (R Sheridan), 20 (R Sheridan), 21 top (R Sheridan), 23 (R Sheridan), 25 top (R R Bell), 29 (Mary Jelliffe); Corbis 31 (Hulton Deutsch); Corbis Digital Stock 2, 19, 27; C M Dixon back cover right, 3, 8, 9 top, 11 top, 12 top, 13, 18 both, 21 bottom, 22 top, 24 top, 28; Topham Picturepoint 14, 24–25 (John G Ross), 26; Werner Forman Archive 7 bottom (Dr E Strouhal), 9 bottom (British Museum, London), 15 both (Egyptian Museum, Cairo), 17 top (Egyptian Museum, Cairo), 22 bottom (Egyptian Museum, Cairo). Artwork by Michael Posen.

◀ *The Temple of Amun at Luxor. The statues are of the pharaoh Ramses II (see page 19).*

CONTENTS

▶ *This container, called a canopic jar, held the stomach of a person who had been mummified (see page 22).*

MEET THE EGYPTIANS

In some ways the ancient Egyptians were like any other people. But they also behaved in ways that some people today see as strange. One of the strangest things was that they were able to live in Egypt at all.

Egypt is a dry, hot country with very little rainfall. Most of the land is desert. The only reason that people were able to live in Egypt in ancient times was the strange behaviour of the River Nile, which runs through Egypt. Each year, between July and October, the River Nile flooded. It covered the land beside the river. When the water went down, it left a thick layer of mud behind. This mud was the only soil in Egypt that could grow crops. The ancient Egyptians called the desert 'the red land' and the mud from the Nile 'the black land'.

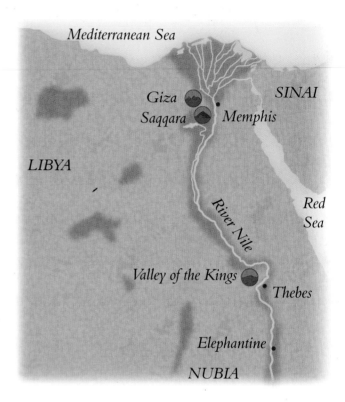

▲ This map of Egypt shows the land where crops could grow shaded in green.

► Some Egyptian craftsmen were very skilled at making beautiful jewellery, such as this collar in the shape of a vulture.

The ancient Egyptians also hunted fish and birds on the river. They grew reeds along the riverbank to make boats, baskets and paper. The fastest way to travel was on the river, too.

Most people say the ancient Egyptian civilization began in about 3100 BC. The ancient Egyptians began to settle by the River Nile about 4000 years ago. They lived there for about 3000 years, until Egypt was taken over and ruled by people from other countries.

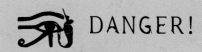 DANGER!

Surprisingly, it was men, not women, who washed the clothes in ancient Egypt. In most other societies, washing was seen as women's work. But in ancient Egypt clothes were washed in the River Nile, which was full of crocodiles. Washing clothes was a dangerous job!

▼ *Although it hardly rains in Egypt, the Nile floods every year. This happens when heavy rain falls in the mountains far upstream, causing a rush of water down the river.*

MAKING A LIVING

A king, called a pharaoh, ruled ancient Egypt and was the richest and most important person in the country. The least important people were slaves and the poor. Everyone else fitted in between, each on a different level of importance.

The pharaoh was said to have been chosen by the gods. Sometimes the ancient Egyptians even said that the pharaohs were gods. A pharaoh had the most power, but he had to look after everyone in Egypt. This included feeding everyone from his own food stores in the years when crops did not grow very well. He could not run the whole of Egypt by himself. So he chose people called governors to run different parts of the country for him, to make sure his orders were carried out.

 PASS IT ON

Almost everyone in ancient Egypt did the same work their father had done and passed their skills on to their children.

◄ *Scribes spent their whole day writing, but had no desks. They wrote sitting cross-legged with a board across their knees.*

▶ Even now, Egyptians farm the land with tools that are very like those of ancient Eygpt.

The ancient Egyptians expected men and women to do different kinds of jobs. Men were miners, for example, while women wove cloth. Women were not supposed to be pharaohs, but a few were. They dressed like male pharaohs, and even wore a false beard.

Everyone in ancient Egypt had to work for the pharaoh for a set number of days each year, as a kind of tax. Wealthy people often paid someone to do their duty work for them. Often this work was building temples, pyramids or tombs.

▶ Tomb walls show important people doing jobs below their status, such as farming, in their best clothes!

EGYPTIANS AT HOME

 This painting shows how some houses were built on a platform. This was to keep them dry when the River Nile flooded.

All ancient Egyptian homes were built from mud brick, even the pharaoh's palace. The only stone buildings, which were made to last, were temples, pyramids and tombs.

Egypt was very hot all year round. People built homes with thick walls and small high windows to keep out the heat. They painted the walls white to reflect the heat away from the house. Homes had flat roofs, reached by an outside stairway. People spent more time on the roof than inside their homes. They even cooked and ate there. They grew climbing plants over a frame or used a cloth held up by poles to give shade to where they sat.

Richer people had larger homes, with higher ceilings and more than one level. These homes were often built around gardens with a pond. The floors of the homes were simply beaten earth or, for wealthier people, mud-brick tiles.

STRANGE BEDS

Many ordinary homes did not have beds. People slept on raised platforms of mud brick. Wealthier people had wooden beds with woven rushes. They had no pillows, but used a carved wooden neck support.

▶ *Rich people liked to have shady gardens with big ponds.*

▼ *This model of an Egyptian house shows the courtyard, the outside stairs (on the left) to the roof and an air vent in the roof. They are out of scale, but they show the parts of a home that the ancient Egyptians thought were important.*

Inside, the walls were painted white and then decorated. Ordinary people might have several different bands of colour or coloured patterns painted on the walls. Palaces were decorated with scenes from everyday life, such as hunting and fishing.

The ancient Egyptians did not use curtains or blinds, but they did sometimes fix pieces of linen cloth over the windows to keep the insects out. This, and the fact that the windows were small and high, meant homes were often quite dark and airless inside.

FAMILY LIFE

The ancient Egyptians thought families were very important. This was partly because they believed that when people were dead they still needed looking after: food had to be brought to their tombs and prayers said for them. Children and grandchildren were important in order that this care could continue.

► *Ancient Egyptian couples are often shown holding hands. This couple is the pharaoh Akenaten and his wife, Nefertiti.*

 SICK BABIES

One cure for a baby that was sick was for the mother to cook and eat a mouse. The mouse's bones were then cleaned and put into a linen bag. The bag was tied up carefully with seven knots, and the baby wore the bag around its neck until it was well again.

Strangely, although the ancient Egyptians thought families were important, they did not perform complicated ceremonies for weddings or if people got divorced. A couple were seen as starting family life when they set up home together. Often, parents arranged marriages for their children, but if either was unhappy in the marriage they could leave.

Men were expected to look after any wives they divorced, to make sure they had a place to live, food and clothing.

Babies were sometimes named in honour of one of the many ancient Egyptian gods. Many were named after the pharaoh who was ruling at the time. This must have been quite confusing!

Ancient Egyptian children played with balls, skittles and dolls. They played racing games and leapfrog.

Children wore their hair in a long plait on the right side of their heads. This was the 'sidelock of youth' and was cut off when the children were about ten years old. They then had to put their toys away and begin training for adult life.

FOOD AND DRINK

Most of the time the ancient Egyptians ate small meals of vegetables, fish, bread and fruit. However, on special days they had feasts where they were expected to eat and drink a lot, often until they were sick.

The most important foods in Egypt were bread and beer, both made from barley or wheat. Poor people, including the children, ate and drank very little else. Wealthy people sometimes ate meat. Many ancient Egyptians had worn teeth. Sand and grit often got into the flour and wore down the teeth as people ate the bread.

▲ *This is ancient Egyptian wheat, found in a tomb. The ancient Egyptians thought people would go on baking and brewing beer in the afterlife.*

▼ *This tomb model shows servants making bread and beer for a royal palace.*

Bread was cooked in a special bread oven, but most other food was cooked over an open fire, either stewed or boiled in pots or cooked quickly on sticks over the open flames. People ate from clay or wooden bowls or straight from the pot. Everyone ate with their fingers. They poured water over each others' hands to wash them afterwards.

▲ *Geese were kept for their eggs and their meat. Each year, the men who looked after the geese had to bring them to be counted.*

When wealthy people held a feast, the cooks made huge amounts of a wide range of food. Guests ate and drank a lot. As well as bread, vegetables, fish and meat, such as goat or chicken, they ate wild animals. Ducks, geese, herons, cranes and even flamingoes were hunted and then fattened up for the feast.

 BREWING BEER

Beer was made from partly baked bread, barley and water. This was mashed and mixed in jars, left for a few days then strained and drunk. Even after straining, the soggy bread made the beer thick and cloudy. It had to be drunk through a special straw made from lead that held back the thickest lumps.

SICKNESS AND HEALTH

Medical care in ancient Egypt was so good that Egyptian doctors were famous and in demand in many parts of the ancient world. Most doctors were men; some of them were specialists who cared for just one part of the body.

Ancient Egyptian doctors learned by studying ancient medical writings. They used a mixture of magic and herbal medicine to cure a patient, saying a magic spell at the same time as they put ointment on a bad cut, for example. They believed that the magic and the medicine were equally important, and both had to work before the patient was cured.

Some of the ingredients in ancient Egyptian medicine would be considered unusual today. They include lizards' blood, pigs' teeth, rotting meat and stinking fat.

▲ This statue shows Imhotep, who was adviser and doctor to an early Egyptian pharaoh, Djoser. Later, he was worshipped as a god of medicine.

NATURE KNOWS BEST

Several ancient Egyptian herbal cures are very similar to modern ones. For example, the ancient Egyptians gave willow bark and poppy juice to ease pain. These herbal cures have similar chemicals in them to the modern medicines aspirin and morphine used to fight pain today.

The ancient Egyptians had surgeons, dentists and opticians, as well as ordinary doctors. They had vets to look after animals, too. Surgeons mainly healed wounds and set broken and fractured bones. They did not carry out operations to fix problems inside the body. This was against their religious beliefs.

Dentists sometimes put a tooth that had come out back in, fixing it to the tooth next to it with copper wire. They also drilled and filled teeth. Opticians cared for eye infections but did not have the technology to make glasses.

▲ *A carving of Hesire, the chief of Dentists and Doctors under the pharaoh Zoser. He has a scribe set over his shoulder. All doctors had to train to scribe.*

▶ *The ancient Egyptians wore amulets as a magical protection against disease. Some amulets showed a god or goddess with medical powers. Others showed very powerful gods, like this ram amulet of the god Amun. The people who wore them hoped the powerful god would be able to keep away a whole range of the evil spirits that they thought brought disease.*

LOOKING GOOD

Most ancient Egyptians wore clothes made from linen, a cloth woven from the flax plant that grew well in Egypt. The poorest people wore very simple clothes that were easy to move about in. Rich people wore more complicated styles.

Most of the time, people left the linen cloth white to reflect the heat. Usually they cut their hair very short or shaved their heads to keep cool. They wore wigs when they wanted to dress up. Poor people wore wigs made from vegetable fibres, such as the bark of date trees. Rich people wore wigs made from real human hair, which sometimes still had the head lice from the original owner!

Both men and women wore jewellery and make-up, such as eyeliner. Poorer people probably just had a string of beads or a copper bracelet. The ancient Egyptians outlined their eyes with kohl, a black eyepaint. Some people think that this helped against the glare of the sun rather like sunglasses.

▲ *The woman on the left of the picture is wearing a dress of thin linen with lots of pleats. The woman in the tight dress is a goddess.*

 TIGHT DRESSES

Ancient Egyptian artists showed women in very close-fitting clothes that showed off their shape. However many of them would have been impossible to walk in. Clothes from the time, found by archaeologists, suggest women's clothes were looser and more shapeless than their paintings show.

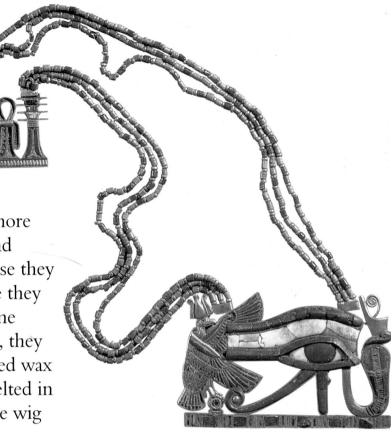

▶ *This necklace belonged to a man, the pharaoh Tutankhamun.*

The richer people were, the more complicated their jewellery and make-up was. This was because they had more money, and because they could spend much of their time indoors in the cool. At parties, they sometimes put cones of scented wax on their heads. As the wax melted in the heat and mixed in with the wig hair, it gave off a nice smell.

◀ *This girl's make-up box had pots for eyeliner, perfume and eyeshadow. She also had several necklaces, a bracelet and an arm ring.*

RELIGION

The ancient Egyptians believed in many different gods and goddesses, each controlling a different part of everyday life. So the god Khepri appeared as a dung beetle each day and slowly rolled the sun across the sky.

Because the gods could interfere in people's lives, the ancient Egyptians prayed to them and gave them gifts to keep them happy.

Some gods and goddesses were more important than others and were worshipped in big stone temples all over Egypt. Others were less important and only worshipped in some places. For example Sobek, the Crocodile God, was mostly worshipped in places along the River Nile where lots of crocodiles lived.

▲ *The face of the household god Bes is scary, but he was a kind god. He pulled faces to scare away evil spirits.*

▶ *The ancient Egyptians believed that the jackal headed god, Anubis, would judge the dead. He weighed their heart on a scale against the Feather of Truth. It had to balance.*

ANIMAL-HEADED GODS

Ancient Egyptian gods and goddesses were often shown with human bodies but the heads of the animals sacred to them. The goddess Hathor's sacred animal was the cow. So she was shown as a human with a cow's head, as a cow and, sometimes, as a human with the ears of a cow. Anubis, god of the dead, had the body of a man and the head of a jackal. The god Thoth was shown as a baboon or with the head of an ibis bird.

Strangely, some gods controlled more than one part of life. Gods were given different names for each area of life they influenced. So Re, the Sun God, was also Amun Ra, King of all the Gods. The most important gods and goddesses were worshipped in temples by priests and priestesses. Temples were seen as the homes of the gods, and ordinary people did not worship there but at small shrines, which were set up in towns and along the banks of the Nile.

▶ *The entrance to the Temple of Amun in Luxor is guarded by two statues of the pharaoh Ramses II 16.5m high. That is about the same as nine men standing on each other's shoulders.*

WRITING

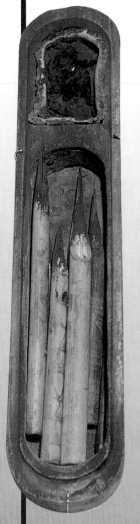

The ancient Egyptians developed writing in about 3100 BC. Egypt was a long, thin country, running along the River Nile, and the pharaoh needed to send written instructions to the officials governing Egypt for him.

The earliest kind of writing was picture writing, called hieroglyphs. Hieroglyphs were very complicated, and soon scribes developed another kind of writing, a simplified kind, called hieratic. This was used for everyday writing. Hieroglyphs were used for everything that had religious meaning and was meant to last, such as on temples, in tombs and on things to go in tombs.

▲ *This is a scribe's pen case and inkwell. Ancient Egyptian artists used many different colours, but scribes used two, black and red. These were used for different purposes. When scribes wrote out calendars they wrote out the 'unlucky' days in red, which they saw as an unlucky colour.*

WRITING BACKWARDS

The ancient Egyptians sometimes wrote from left to right, as we do. But sometimes they wrote from right to left or from top to bottom. It all depended on the space they had to fill and what else was near the writing. So if there was a picture of a person or animal you had to read going towards the eye of the person or animal.

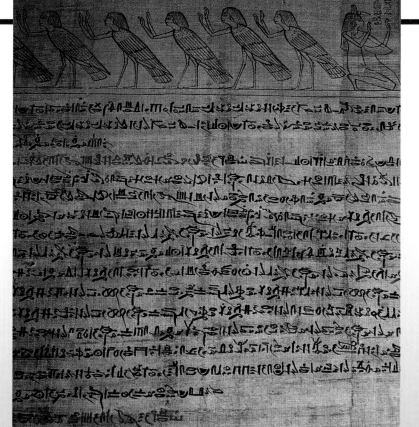

◄ *This papyrus is written in demotic writing.*

▼ *The pharaoh usually sent his orders by messenger, or on papyrus scrolls. But one pharaoh, Amenhotep III, kept his scribes busy carving scarab stones to send to all his governors. The news on the stones included a list of Amenhotep's skill at hunting – including killing 107 lions in the first 10 years of his reign.*

Artists had to learn how to draw hieroglyphs exactly. They also had to learn the meaning of the various colours that were used to paint the hieroglyphs. Each colour had a special meaning. For example, green was the colour of death. As the ancient Egyptians used writing more and more for record keeping, instructions, reports, even ordinary letter writing, they simplified hieratic writing even more. This new kind of writing was called demotic. Many ordinary people who were not scribes understood some demotic. By the end of the ancient Egyptian period, writing was no longer just something that scribes did.

Mummies

The ancient Egyptians believed in a life after death where people would need their bodies. So they tried hard to preserve bodies after death. One way was to wrap the body in layers of bandages, making what we now call mummies.

Before the mummies were wrapped, the bodies were embalmed to preserve them. Embalming became a special job, done outside in tents with open sides to let the wind take the smells away. Embalmers took out the soft body organs, including the brain, which they pulled out through the nose with copper hooks. They left the heart inside. They covered the body with a salt called natron, which soaked up body fluids. Then they wrapped the body in bandages soaked in oil.

Embalmers charged different rates for different levels of care. Pharaohs lay in natron for 70 days and they were wrapped in about 400 sq m of the best linen, cut into strips of different widths and lengths. Poorer people lay in natron for less time and were often wrapped in old linen clothes or sheets. One man was found wrapped in a sail from a boat.

◀ *The golden death mask of the pharaoh Psusennes Io.*

▲ *The liver, lungs, stomach and intestines of the dead person were kept in special jars called canopic jars. This jar, with a jackal headed lid, he the stomac*

The reconstructed face of the pharaoh Tutankhamun. It was damaged when it was unwrapped.

Once a mummy was wrapped, it was given a mask over the face, called a death mask, and placed in a wooden mummy case. Depending on how important the dead person was, it might have several mummy cases and even a stone coffin, called a sarcophagus.

CURSE OF THE MUMMY

So many people died after the tomb of Tutankhamun was excavated that stories began to spread that Tutankhamun had cursed the people who had opened his tomb. The curse was making them die!

PYRAMIDS AND TOMBS

Because the ancient Egyptians believed in an afterlife, they buried people carefully, with many possessions. The most important people were the pharaohs so they were buried with the most care and the most valuable possessions.

▲ *Sculptors made beautiful carvings in stone and wood, as well as tomb models, to put in tombs.*

We do not know how the earliest pharaohs were buried, but from about 2650 to 2400 BC, they were buried in pyramids. Pyramids took a lot of time and effort to build and were a sign of the power of the pharaoh. But they were also very obvious to tomb robbers. Traps, false passages and blocked entrances were built into the pyramids, and the walls were very thick. Despite all this, every pyramid was broken into and robbed in ancient times. All the precious jewellery, perfumes, furniture and other possessions were stolen. After 2400 BC, ancient Egyptian pharaohs were buried in tombs, not pyramids.

▼ *The pyramids at Giza. Strangely, the one that looks the tallest is not. It was just built on a higher piece of ground.*

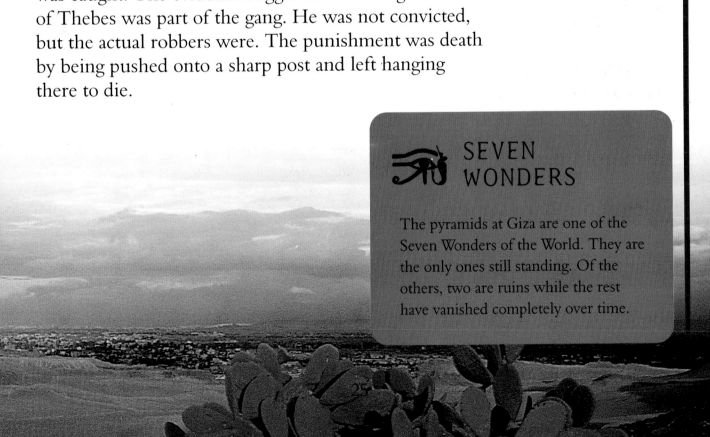

▶ Tombs dug into rock are hard to spot, hard to get into, and easy to guard. It is surprising, then, that tomb robbers managed to find, break into and rob almost all of them.

The Valley of the Kings is one of the most famous burial places. Unlike the pyramids, the Valley of the Kings did not make it obvious where the royal tombs were. There was only one small entrance for each tomb, and the burial ground had special police guarding it. Despite this, only one tomb was not robbed – the tomb of Tutankhamun, found in 1922.

Tomb robbers were not usually caught. Those who were, often turned out to be tomb workers or relatives of tomb workers. In about 1108 BC a tomb-robbing gang was caught. The evidence suggested that the governor of Thebes was part of the gang. He was not convicted, but the actual robbers were. The punishment was death by being pushed onto a sharp post and left hanging there to die.

SEVEN WONDERS

The pyramids at Giza are one of the Seven Wonders of the World. They are the only ones still standing. Of the others, two are ruins while the rest have vanished completely over time.

25

EGYPTIAN FACTS

Here is a selection of interesting facts about the strange world of the Egyptians.

IMPOSSIBLE ART

Ancient Egyptian art had lots of rules, including rules about how you painted people. For example, men were painted with a darker skin than women. People had to be sideways on, but they also had to show both shoulders. So people sit and stand with their legs and heads sideways, but their body from the waist to the neck facing forwards. This is uncomfortable, if not impossible!

CARE AFTER DEATH

In 1975, Egyptologists unwrapping a girl's mummy discovered she had been unwrapped before, in ancient times. The ancient Egyptians who had unwrapped her had found her legs broken and her feet smashed. Because they believed she needed her body in the afterlife, they made her feet from clay and reeds and fixed them to her legs with splints. Then they wrapped her up again.

PRACTICE MAKES PERFECT

Almost all ancient Egyptian pyramids are perfect in size and shape. However the builders of one pyramid, at Dashur, got their calculations wrong and began building so the sides sloped at an angle of 54 degrees. By the time they were halfway up, they saw that when the sides met they would not be strong enough to hold themselves up! So they changed to working at 43 degrees, to reach a point sooner.

GREAT INVENTIONS

The ancient Egyptians were the first people we know to use umbrellas, the 365-day year, locks, rulers, zoos, the police, the lighthouse, maps and mathematical calculations of angles, heights and distances.

◄ *The artist here has followed the rules showing the tomb owner as biggest with dark skin. Both he and his wife have both shoulders facing out.*

MEETING THE GODS

In ancient Egyptian temples, the priests and priestesses cared for a statue of the god of the temple, washing, dressing and offering it food each day. The statue was always kept in a low, dark shrine at the far end of the temple. All priests could use the first courtyard of the temple, but fewer of them could go into the other courtyards between the entrance and the shrine. Only the most important priest could go into the shrine itself.

WHY NO CARTS?

The ancient Egyptians had wheeled chariots to fight from when they went to war. However, they did not use wheels on anything else. There were no carts to carry things or people from place to place.

SPHINX

The Sphinx at Giza guards the pyramid of Khafra. It is carved from a lump of hard-wearing rock. There is a story that Khafra had it made because he had decided to build his pyramid behind the rock, on the highest ground in Giza, so that it looked bigger than the Great Pyramid of his father. He carved the Sphinx out of the rock so that it would look good in front of his tomb.

▼ *The Sphinx at Giza.*

EGYPTIAN WORDS

This glossary explains some of the words used in this book that you might not have seen before.

▼ *The ancient Egyptians put hieroglyphs everywhere, even squeezing them into gaps around pictures.*

Afterlife
The place where the ancient Egyptians believed the dead went to live.

Amulet
A small magic symbol, worn to keep a person safe.

Desert
A dry place, which has little or no rain all year.

Egyptologists
People who study ancient Egypt.

Embalming
Preserving dead bodies from decay by making them into mummies.

Governor
A person who ruled part of ancient Egypt for the pharaoh, living there and making sure the pharaoh's orders were carried out.

Hieroglyphs
Ancient Egyptian picture writing.

Miner
A person who digs something valuable, such as coal, copper or gold, out of the ground.

Mummies
Bodies of dead people that have been preserved.

Official
A person chosen to work for the pharaoh. Officials made sure the pharaoh's orders were carried out.

Pharaoh
Ruler of ancient Egypt, usually a man.

Priest/priestess

A person who worked in a temple, serving a god or goddess.

Sacred

Something is sacred if it is important or special to a religion.

Scribes

The only people in ancient Egypt who could read and write. They did all the record keeping.

▼ *The ancient Egyptians filled their tombs with things they would need in the afterlife. Here, servants carry furniture into a tomb.*

Shrine

A place where the statue of a god or goddess is kept so that people can pray to it and care for it as if it were the god or goddess.

Slaves

People who were treated by their owners as property. They could be bought and sold and were not free to leave.

Temple

A home for a god or goddess where their image is cared for by priests and priestesses.

Tomb

A place where someone is buried.

EGYPTIAN PROJECTS

WRITE IN HIEROGLYPHS

Hieroglyphs were very complicated and could be put together to mean lots of different things. But the alphabet is a good start! There is not a symbol for every letter of the alphabet, so we have put that letter with the letter that sounds closest to it. Make your name from the hieroglyphs on this page.

▼ *Write out your name using these hieroglyphs. At the end of your name draw the female sign if you are a girl, or the male sign if you are a boy.*

A ... or ...   H ... or ...   O ...   V ...

B ...   I ...   P ...   W ...

C ... or ...   J ...   Q ...   X ... or ...

D ...   K ...   R ...   Y ... or ...

E ...   L ...   S ...   Z ...

F ...   M ...   T ...

G ...   N ...   U ...

SH ...   CH ...   KH ...

male   female

▶ *This photo shows the discovery of Tutankhamun's tomb in 1922.*

FIND OUT ABOUT THE TOMB OF TUTANKHAMUN

Use websites and books from your local library to find out about the discovery of Tutankhamun's tomb in 1922. Try searching using the word 'Tutankhamun'.

MAKE A MUMMY

If you have, or can borrow, a small doll you could turn it into a mummy using strips of toilet paper, tissue paper or even scraps of cloth. Before making your mummy, experiment with the paper or cloth to find the easiest way to work with it. Are long, thin strips better than short fat ones? What is the best way to wind, close together and overlapping or far apart?

VISIT A MUMMY

Many museums have Egyptian collections, including mummies. In Britain, the British Museum, London, the Ashmolean Museum in Oxford and the Manchester Museum have large collections. In the USA, visit the Smithsonian Institution in Washington, DC and the Oriental Institute, Chicago.

EGYPTIANS ON THE INTERNET

Surfing the Internet is the quickest way to find out information about the Egyptians. But the Internet is constantly changing so if you can't find these websites try searching using the word 'Egyptians'.

www.ancientegypt.co.uk
A site run by the British Museum that covers all aspects of life in ancient Egypt.

www.touregypt.net
The official website of the Egyptian Ministry of Tourism. It has some good information and some excellent pictures.

www.pbs.org/wgbh/nova/egypt
Some of the text is hard to read, but there is lots of information, pictures and diagrams.

INDEX